# CONTENTS

Stories by Maureen Spurgeon

First published 1998
by Brown Watson, England

ISBN: 0-7097-1258-8
© 1998 Brown Watson, England
Printed in the E.C.

# CHRISTMAS

## COLLECTION

### Book Four

*Brown Watson*

ENGLAND

# SANTA'S
# BUSY DAY

Illustrated by Stephen Holmes

Santa had been very busy all morning, getting ready for Christmas Eve!

"Have a rest, Santa!" cried an elf. "You're always so busy!"

"But I LIKE being busy!" said Santa. "And do you know the job I like best of all?"

"Riding the sleigh!" said the elf.
"Putting all the toys in sacks!"
cried the Christmas Fairy.
"Wrong!" laughed Santa.
"What I like best is reading all
my letters."

"Your letters!" cried the little Christmas elf. "That reminds me! Has anyone written asking for a little wooden engine, Santa? This one gets left behind every Christmas Eve."

"I don't think so..." said Santa. "Can you put it in my sack? I really MUST read these letters. They're from children in the town I'm visiting tomorrow!" Suddenly, he stopped.

Dec 20

"Listen to this!" he said.
"Dear Santa, will you please bring an extra nice present as a Christmas surprise for our daddy. Thank you. Lots of love from Tina and Tom!"

"If only Tina and Tom had said what they wanted for their daddy!" groaned Santa. "How do I know what he would like?" "What about some hankies?" said the Christmas Fairy.

"That doesn't sound much of a surprise!" said Santa. Then Penny Pixie, who helped look after the reindeer, had an idea.
"What about one of your Christmas beakers?" she said.

Santa Claus gave a big smile. "Now that's a REAL Christmas surprise!" he said.
"I can't wait to see Tina and Tom's faces when I meet their daddy tomorrow!"

Very early the next morning,
Santa got ready to begin his long
journey. "Wrap up warmly!" said
Penny, tucking a scarf inside his
cloak. "You're sure to have a very
busy day!"

It was still dark when the town
where Tina and Tom lived came
in sight. "Put me down beside
that big Christmas tree," Santa
told the reindeer, "and then you
can take the sleigh back home!"

Soon, Santa knew, he would be busy meeting people and hearing what everyone wanted for Christmas! He was looking forward to seeing Tom and Tina with their daddy.

He didn't have long to wait.
"Look, Daddy!" someone cried,
and a girl and a boy came
hurrying up. "Tina and Tom!"
smiled Santa. "Here's that
Christmas surprise for Daddy!"

"We're Mike and Mandy, not Tina and Tom!" said the boy. "And I'm Paddy, their big brother!" said the man. "But thanks for the surprise, Santa! It's just what I've always wanted!"

"Oh, no!" thought poor Santa. "What can I give Tina and Tom's daddy, now?" Just then, up came another boy and girl, with someone wearing a crash helmet and motorbike leggings.

"Come on Tom!" cried the girl.
"Tom!" thought Santa. "Tom and
Tina with their daddy!" Without
thinking, he unwound the scarf
from inside his cloak and handed
it across.

"Here's a Christmas surprise for you, sir!" he cried. "A very merry Christmas!" Tom gave a cheer. "Just what Sam wanted!" he cried. "She looks after us."

"Sam?" echoed Santa Claus.

The person took off the crash helmet with a shake of her long, fair hair. "A scarf!" she cried. "Just the thing when I'm riding my motorbike, eh, kids?" And Sam gave Santa a big kiss!

So many people wanted to see Santa Claus on that busy day! Everyone looked so pleased and so happy, he could not help smiling. But at the same time, he was also very worried.

Santa had been so busy, giving out lots of lovely things from his sack, that soon there would be nothing left at all!
"Oh dear!" thought poor Santa Claus. "Whatever shall I do?"

"Hello, Santa!" someone said, and Santa Claus turned to see a girl in a bobble hat. "I'm Tina and this is my brother, Tom! Did you get our letter about a surprise for our daddy?"

"Er, well..." Santa stopped, and without thinking, he put his hand deep into his sack, feeling around at the very bottom. There was something small and hard, tucked away in one corner.

It was the little wooden engine!
Tom and Tina's daddy gave a big
smile, reaching out to touch it.
"A model engine!" he cried. "I've
always wanted a  model engine!
Thank you, Santa!"

"You ARE clever, Santa!" said
Tina. "Tom SAID you'd know what
Daddy wanted!" Tom looked very
proud. And their daddy? He just
kept looking at the little wooden
engine!

Santa was chuckling all the way home! "Why did I worry about that Christmas surprise?" he kept saying. "I only had to remember that grown-ups never quite stop being children!"

It was soon dark. Snow began
falling and Santa was glad to see
the lights from his workshop.
"I'll be glad to have a rest!" he
told his reindeer. "I've had SUCH
a busy day!"

33

# THE CHRISTMAS ELF

Illustrated by Mimi Everett

Everyone in Santa Claus' little workshop had to agree — Eddie the elf was really a very nice person. He was always smiling and cheerful — never cross or grumpy. And he was always ready to help.

"I'll carry that!" he cried when he saw Dame Jolly bringing in the teacups. "Give your arms a rest."

Poor Eddie! He didn't mean to
make Dame Jolly spill the tea!
"Oh, Eddie . . ." she sighed.
"Don't worry!" grinned Eddie –
something he often said when
things went wrong. I'll soon wipe
it up."

"Oh dear, no!" groaned Fixit the handyman. "Not with my brand new sack!"

"Sorry!" grinned Eddie – something else he often said. "I'll wash it."

"No, wait!" cried Fixit. "There are some toy cars inside!"

SMASH! Eddie thought it was a good idea to tip the cars out on to the floor!

CRASH! Down fell Pink the Pixie and Maid Merry!

"Sorry . . ." said Eddie, again.

"That's what you always say," groaned Fixit. "Did you remember to take over that box of spinning tops Santa Claus wanted?"
"Sorry!" gasped Eddie. "I forgot."

Just then, Santa Claus came in.
He did not look very pleased.
"All the paintboxes have been
mixed up with the skittles!" he
said. "Who packed this sack?"
"Sorry . . ." said Eddie.

"Humph! You can't carry on like this, Eddie," grunted Santa Claus, looking around at the mess.
"Sorry," said poor Eddie.
"I really do mean to help".

"I know, I know," said Santa Claus. "Try and help Tolly, the Teddy Bear maker, will you?" Eddie just nodded in reply. He knew he had to show that he could work well. And Tolly did need help.

"Er, just start tidying up for now," said Tolly, when Eddie asked what he could do to help.
"I've got to try and get so many Teddy Bears finished and packed up before Christmas Eve."

Kind-hearted Eddie did feel sorry for him. Suppose, he thought, just suppose he made some Teddy Bears for Tolly. Santa Claus would know what a good helper he was, then!

He was soon busy, cutting and
stitching, snipping and sewing.
The seams were a bit crooked
and one ear looked bigger than
the other, but Eddie was very
pleased with his work!

"Only the thread to cut, now," he
thought. Instead, he cut a big
hole in one paw! But he soon cut
a patch of material to stick on
top. He had just finished when
Tolly gave a shout.

"Where's that piece of sparkly fur
I left here? That's all I had!"
"Oh, don't worry about that,"
said Eddie. "See what I've made."
"Th-that patch!" choked Tolly.
"It's cut from my special fur!"

"Sorry . . ." said Eddie.
"Sorry?" cried Tolly. "I've got to
finish off a batch of Teddy Bears!"
Santa Claus came in to see what
all the shouting was about, his
face was grim and unsmiling.

"I'm going to a big shop in town, tomorrow," he said at last. "You can come with me, Eddie. If you can find any child who really wants that Teddy Bear, I'll let you stay in my workshop."

Eddie the elf had never been inside a big shop, before.

The first person to come and see Santa Claus was a mummy with two children – and Eddie was sure the baby would love the Teddy Bear .

But each time he tried to give it to the baby, she kept throwing it on the floor! In the end, it got so dusty and dirty that Eddie decided to try putting it in a Christmas stocking he saw hanging on the wall.

"Here!" cried one of the shop assistants. "Who's put this old thing in our Christmas display? I'll put it out with the rubbish."

"No, wait!" shouted Eddie the elf. "You can't do that!"

Santa Claus frowned across at Eddie. All the noise had upset a little girl and made her cry. The only thing Eddie could do now was search through the rubbish and just hope he would find the Teddy Bear . . .

And what a state the Teddy Bear was in! Dirty patches on his fur, stitches coming undone, bits of stuffing oozing out . . . who would want it, now? Eddie picked it up and went outside . . .

"Bear!" cried a little voice and a hand reached out. "Nice bear! Look, Mummy! Like Patchy!"

"No, darling," said the little girl's mummy. "It doesn't belong to you!"

"I'm sorry," the lady went on. "You see, Janey left her old rag doll on the bus last week, and it's made her so unhappy. She didn't even want the lovely, new doll Santa Claus tried to give her!"

"I thought I was the one who had made her cry," said Eddie. Janey's mummy just laughed.

"No!" she said. "You've made her smile." And Janey actually gave the Teddy Bear a big kiss!

Eddie smiled for the first time that day. And, when he said Janey could keep the bear she wanted so much, she and her mummy could not stop smiling. "Merry Christmas!" cried Eddie.

"Merry Christmas!" cried Janey. "And thank you for my present!"

"Well done, Eddie," murmured Santa Claus. "Now, it's time for us to go. There's still lots of work to do before Christmas Eve!"

# THE
# CHRISTMAS
# SNOWMAN

*Illustrated by Colin Petty*

"It's cold enough for snow!" said Simon and Julie's dad, as he took one last look out at their back garden. Then he locked the door for the night.

"I hope not!" said Mum, who was busy baking Christmas cake and mince pies. I really hate going Christmas shopping when it's snowy and cold."

All the same, Simon and Julie couldn't help wishing that it WOULD snow – even if it was just enough to build a snowman for Christmas! And when they woke up next day – what do you think?

Roofs of houses and garden sheds, window sills and fences were powdered with snow, sparkling in the winter sunshine like icing sugar. "Great!" Simon cried. "We can build a snowman."

"You'll have to be quick!" laughed Dad. "We didn't have much snow, and it won't last long."
"Good!" said Mum, mixing the cake. "I'm glad," added Gran.

The children put on their coats, wellingtons, woolly hats and gloves and went outside. "It's true what Dad says," sighed Julie looking around. "There isn't really all that much snow . . ."

"I think there's enough by the wall," Simon told her, scooping up quite a few handfuls. "See if you can make a big snowball for the head, and I'll start on the snowman's body."

Julie found that getting enough snow even to make a little snowball was not easy. Scraping the whole of the garden fence only gave her a tiny handful, and most of that was already melting.

Simon had not done much better with the snowman's body. And if Mum hadn't opened an upstairs window, sending down a shower of snow, they would not have managed to finish him, at all.

"He's a bit small . . ." said Julie.
"Don't worry!" said Simon. "We can always make him bigger, as long as we get some more snow before Christmas. Let's call him Snowy, the Christmas Snowman!"

The weather stayed quite cold,
but there was no more snow.
"At least I can hang out some
washing," said Mum.
"And I can do some Christmas
shopping," smiled Gran.

Julie and Simon were very disappointed.

"Oh, don't worry about your snowman," Dad told them. "That wall gets hardly any sun, you know. He'll last until Christmas."

But there was no mistake about it. Snowy was getting smaller and smaller. And the smaller he got, the easier it became for the pale, winter sun to melt more and more of him away.

If it had not been for Jack Frost coming round every night and touching everything with his long, icy fingers, Snowy knew he would never have lasted so long.

Everyone else seemed so happy.
Fairy lights appeared in all the
windows. Snowy could hear Julie
and Simon laughing and chatting
as they helped to put up the
decorations.

"Time to mix the Christmas pudding!" came Mum's voice. "Take it in turns to make a wish!" "I'd wish to be a real Christmas snowman!" thought Snowy.

Snowy glanced up at the dark sky, hoping he'd see clouds gathering around him, hiding the moon before the first snowflakes drifted down. Instead, it was a clear night, with lots of stars.

He looked again. Something was gliding towards the moon, something piled high, with a man in boots and a hood, pulled by animals with what looked like tree branches on their heads . . .

"Reindeer . . ." whispered Snowy. Simon and Julie had talked a lot about Santa Claus and what they hoped he would bring them on his sleigh. Snowy knew he came from a land of ice and snow . . .

"I wish Santa Claus could bring me some snow," thought poor Snowy. He closed his eyes tight, not wanting to see anything to remind him of the happy time Christmas was meant to be.

At first, Snowy thought he was

dreaming. Something soft began falling on his face, his head, then his body. It fluttered all around him like a shower of bright moonbeams, making him feel warm and happy . . .

"Snow!" cried Snowy joyfully. "Merry Christmas!" came the cry from above. "Merry Christmas, Snowy!" And in a final burst of stars and moonbeams, both reindeer and sleigh were gone.

"Well, I got just what I wanted for Christmas," said Dad in his new dressing gown. "So did we!" cried Julie and Simon. "Except for our Christmas snowman," added Julie solemnly.

"Well," said Grandma, standing at the back door. "I don't know about that. See for yourselves, you two!" Simon and Julie looked at each other, sure that there had been no snow at all.

Snowy, the Christmas snowman stood proud and tall. His head was round and jolly, and his body so plump and cuddly that Julie could not help giving him a hug for Christmas morning.

"Where did all the snow come from?" they wondered. "And why isn't there snow anywhere else?" When Julie said that it might have something to do with Santa Claus, how they all laughed!

## Stories I have read

Christmas on the Farm ☐

Santa's Little Helper ☐

The Christmas Fairy ☐

The Night Before Christmas ☐

Santa's Busy Day ☐